The Alpha Series

WORKBOOK

John Glenn and Jim Groth

"In that day you shall know that I am in My Father, and you in Me, and I in you."

John 14:20

AuthorHouse™ *AuthorHouse*™ *UK Ltd.*
1663 Liberty Drive, Suite 200 *500 Avebury Boulevard*
Bloomington, IN 47403 *Central Milton Keynes, MK9 2BE*
www.authorhouse.com *www.authorhouse.co.uk*
Phone: 1-800-839-8640 *Phone: 08001974150*

©*2006 John Glenn and Jim Groth. All rights reserved.*

No part of this book may be reproduced, stored in a retrieval system, or transmitted by any means without the written permission of the author.

First published by AuthorHouse 10/23/06

ISBN: 1-4259-6979-8 (sc)

Library of Congress Control Number: 2006909159

Printed in the United States of America
Bloomington, Indiana

This book is printed on acid-free paper.

Alpha Series

DEDICATED TO:

All who are seeking to know the truth about their new identity in Christ

Alpha Series

Acknowledgments:

A special thanks to Jim Groth for his unselfish and tireless efforts to develop this workbook for the advancement of the gospel of grace.

Alpha Series

Preface

For over eighteen years I have taught the Alpha Series to a variety of people in many different settings. Those who begin to understand how the gospel of grace impacts their personal and relational lives immediately see the need to process and apply that message. For that reason this workbook has been developed as a practical tool students can use to help build a healthy identity in Christ. By completing the work in each chapter, we are hoping you will begin to process the truths necessary for personal liberty and relational responsibility.

Each chapter of the workbook corresponds to the chapers of the written text by the same name. Both the manual and the corresponding workbook follow the same basic outline:

I. Biblical Self-Awareness (Chapters 1-4)
II. Our New Identity in Christ (Chapters 5-9)
III. Relational Ministry (Chapters 10-12)

Although each lesson has been designed to offer the student some truth in itself, the best use of the workbook is a progressive study of the principles in the sequence presented. The information gained in the earlier lessons are meant to find application in the later lessons.

It is our hope that this workbook will be used of God to assist you in both understanding and applying the gospel of grace to your own life and the lives of those you love. Please feel free to contact us with comments and questions at www.alphaministries.org.

We look forward to what God is doing in and through you.

John Glenn and Jim Groth

July 2006

Alpha Series

Alpha Series

Table Of Contents

CHAPTER 1: BIBLICAL SELF-AWARENESS- ------ 9
    WHO AM I? ------ 9
    FOUNDATIONS FOR FAMILY LIFE ------ 15

CHAPTER 2: FOUNDATION OF OUR NEEDS ------ 25
    JESUS MEETS OUR PERSONAL NEEDS ------ 25
    OUR UNION WITH CHRIST ------ 33

CHAPTER 3: UNDERSTANDING OUR EMOTIONS ------ 39
    CATEGORIES OF EMOTION ------ 39
    EMOTIONAL HEALING ------ 47

CHAPTER 4: THE HEART OF THE PROBLEM ------ 53
    TRADITIONS OF MEN ------ 53
    HOW PROBLEMS DEVELOP ------ 59

CHAPTER 5: OUR TRUE IDENTITY ------ 69
    GOD'S REGENERATION PROGRAM ------ 69
    THE PROMISE OF VICTORY ------ 77

CHAPTER 6: THE MIRROR ------ 81
    THE OLD AND NEW COVENANTS ------ 81
    SLAVES TO RIGHTEOUSNESS ------ 87

CHAPTER 7: WHO SHALL DELIVER ME? ------ 93
    DEAD TO THE LAW ------ 93
    CONFLICT WITHOUT CONDEMNATION ------ 101

CHAPTER 8: SALVATION BY GRACE ------ 107
    THE FREEDOM OF THE SPIRIT ------ 107
    THE CALL TO FAITH ------ 113

CHAPTER 9: THE COMFORT OF THE SPIRIT ------ 119
    PERSONAL ASSURANCE OF THE SPIRIT ------ 119
    FACING TRIALS IN THE SPIRIT ------ 123

CHAPTER 10: ANOTHER COMFORTER — 129
    RELATIONAL MINISTRY — 129
    COMFORT IN RELATIONAL MINISTRY — 133

CHAPTER 11: ABIDING IN CHRIST — 137
    THE VINE AND THE BRANCHES — 137
    LIVING IN CHRIST'S LOVE — 141

CHAPTER 12: THE OVERCOMER — 145
    THE MINISTRY OF THE OVERCOMER — 145
    THE OVERCOMER'S CHURCH — 149

Biblical Self-Awareness

Who Are you?

Chapter 1
Lesson 1

Identity

Who am I?

This is a simple but very profound question that we each *must* face *daily*. It's simple because it may be answered by supplying things like our name, our occupation, our race, our nationality, or some other general designation or label. However, it is very profound as well. The deeper we probe for an *accurate* answer the more we each must learn about ourselves, and our own sense of identity. This can be painful, but if we are to know the deepest and truest sense of our identity, it must be done.

If you meet someone for the first time, how would you introduce yourself?

How do you think someone close to you (spouse, family member, close friend) would identify you?

Biblical-Self-Awareness - Who Am I?

Deep inside yourself, as you look in, how do you identify yourself?

___

Proverbs 23:7 (KJV or NKJV) Write it down:

Look up Proverbs 23:7, use the KJV or the NKJV. Write down the first phrase.

What does this mean to you?

___

A self-fulfilling prophecy

Based upon what we've discussed so far, how many ways are there of identifying you? Or put another way, how many ways are we seen? Try to state this in broad categories. One is already done:

How others see me
___

Take a look at the picture below:

<u>Personality theorist Carl Rodgers says</u>

Inner turmoil and conflict occurs when **our self-image is different** from that of others or who we really are.

The greater the difference:
- ✔ The greater the inner turmoil.
- ✔ The greater the dysfunction in our lives.

Images

Self — Others — Real

10

Biblical-Self-Awareness - Who Am I?

What comes to mind as you think about this picture?

_____
_____

The greater the difference between how we see ourselves, how others see us, and how we really are; the greater the inner turmoil, and ultimately, the dysfunction in our lives. Likewise, the closer our own self-image lines up with who we really are, and ultimately, how others see us, the less inner conflict we experience, and the healthier we become.

> The closer the self-image lines up with the other two, the healthier we are.

Look up Genesis 2:7. How does this fit into the puzzle of identification?

_____
_____

> **Genesis 2:7**
> **Write it down:**

What is it about our own self image that is so important?

_____
_____
_____

> The key to a healthier more functional life:
>
> Lining up our own self-image with whom God says we really are.

The main purpose of the Alpha Series is to answer the question, "Who Am I?" with biblical truth that provides a solid foundation for a healthier self image and a functional joy filled life.

The Structure of Man

To begin to discover our true identity, we must look at how God made us.
Based upon Genesis 2:7, what are the three main factors?

1. _____
2. _____
3. _____

> We are set free to relate more honestly.
> **Body**
> Physical - houses the spirit being - complex structure of cells, tissues, organs and systems that work together to sustain life.
> **Soul**
> Interaction - between the body and the spirit - personality - *expressed and perceived in our relationships* - the concept of the mind, needs, emotions, and will - development is determined by both physical and spiritual factors.
> **Spirit**
> Immaterial - more than a complex system of electro-chemical reactions - communication with his creator - built-in *God*-consciousness - *self*-consciousness enabling him to discern right from wrong with others.

Look at the chart below and relate the previous three to the chart.

Body
Physical - houses the spirit being - complex structure of cells, tissues, organs and systems that work together to sustain life

Soul
Interaction - between the body and the spirit - personality - *expressed and perceived in our relationships* - the concept of the mind, needs, emotions, and will - development is determined by both physical and spiritual factors

Spirit
Immaterial - more than a complex system of electrochemical reactions - communication with his creator - built-in *God*-consciousness - *self*-consciousness enabling him to discern right from wrong

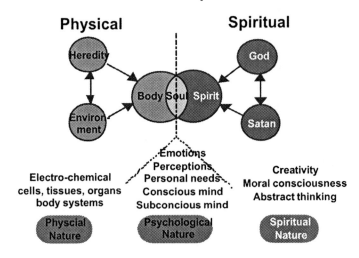

The body, soul, and spirit of man are to be viewed as a very complex system of interactions between each of the components. The body comprises the physical nature, the soul reveals the personal nature, and the spirit constitutes the spiritual nature; all a constant dynamic interaction we call life.

Looking at the "Structure of Man" chart, describe the body component.

Describe the spirit component.

Describe the soul component.

Considering that we are complex beings, of three basic components, influenced by many factors, how do think this affects our problems?

Look up John 2:25.

Who is to be glorified, man or God? _____

Why?

Because of Christ's redemption, I am an awesome spirit being of magnificent worth as a person.

What does this statement mean and why is it true?

**John 2:25
Write it down:**

The study of man from a biblical point of view is intended to, ultimately, impress us with the **magnificence of God.**

Mankind has **a unique potential to reveal and glorify God** as did the "Son of Man" during his earthly ministry.

The Good News

God:

✔ Provides a brand new identity in himself.
✔ Is awesome in our relationship to him.
✔ Calls us to himself as family

Biblical-Self-Awareness - Who Am I?

> The structure of man helps to explain **the difficulty inherent in confronting or changing the basic personality** of human beings.
>
> Explain why:
>
> _____
> _____
> _____
> _____
>
> ### Man cannot change or help himself
>
> Correctional institutions, rehabilitation programs, and mental hospitals reveal the inability of man to fully understand, much less change, himself.

To the extent that we may begin to understand the complexities of ourselves as God's creations, we begin to be more impressed with our God. While humanistic philosophies and religions worship the creature (man) instead of the creator, the study of man from a biblical point of view is intended to ultimately impress us with the magnificence of God. Only an omniscient and sovereign creator could say that, "He needed not that any should testify of man; for he knew what was in man." (John 2:25). As the most complex of all God's creatures, mankind has a unique potential to reveal and glorify God as did the "Son of Man" during his earthly ministry. A truly biblical self-awareness will not only encourage us, but will also glorify God.

Biblical Self-Awareness

The Biblical Foundations for Family Life

**Chapter 1
Lesson 2**

The Divine Family

In thinking about our identity, think about your last name. What does this say about your identity?

How significant is our family of origin, in the physical realm, in determining our identity?

Biblical-Self-Awareness - The Biblical Foundations for Family Life

In the second chapter of Genesis we are given the story of how God created the family system. From the details of this record we discover how God intended for the family system to function, how the family reflects the full nature of God, and also, how the family became naturally dysfunctional.

Genesis 2:18-25
Write down the highlights:

Look up Genesis 2:18-25.

What did God mean, in verse 18, when he said that it was *not good* for man to be alone? In your answer consider this: Was Adam lonely?

_____
_____
_____

What does this have to do with Adam's purpose for being?

_____
_____

God met all of Adam's needs; he was in perfect communion with God.

What is God's purpose in creating Eve?

_____
_____
_____

Consider the following diagram:

God
(Father) (Son) (Holy Spirit)

Attributes
Father Children Mother

Family

Biblical-Self-Awareness - The Biblical Foundations for Family Life

Explain the previous diagram:

Define the Trinity: (Consider the uniqueness of each person, and the unity of God, and the relationships in the Trinity)

> The Trinity consists of the Father, the Son, and the Holy Spirit

To faithfully reveal the completeness of God, what must happen? Consider Adam, Eve, and what they must do.
1.
2.
3.

What is God's purpose for the family?

Principles of Family Living

Refer to Genesis 2:20.
Why was no other creature suitable as a helper for Adam?

> **The Relationship Principle**
>
> Death to self must occur . . .
>
> Adam had to "die" for Eve
>
> What does this foreshadow about the "old man" and the "new man?"

Refer to Genesis 2:21-24.
Why must Eve come from Adam himself?

What does the deep sleep of Adam, symbolically, if not literally illustrate about our relationships with our spouse?

What is another interpretation of the "rib" that God took to fashion Eve?

Men and Women

Which of the following is true or false: (Consider the Trinity when you answer).

Men are more important then women?____
Women are more important than men?____
Men are in charge of women?____
Men and women are different but equal?____

Look at the following diagram:

Leadership through service — Adam ↔ Eve — **Love and Respect**

(Adam / The Family)

Can a man maintain leadership over his family without sacrificial service?

What is sacrificial service?

What enables the woman to love and respect her husband?

Beside sacrificial leadership, what is the main factor that a man must consider in the leadership of his family, which if is not exercised, he is unqualified to lead? (Consider his relationship to God).

Men
Are designed, by God:
- To respond to the initiative of God, not themselves
- To receive respect from his wife
- To give love to his wife

Women
Are designed, by God:
- To respond to the initiative of her husband, not themselves
- To receive love from her husband
- To give respect to her husband

Genesis 2:23
Write it down:

What is the importance of Adam's statement in verse 23?

The Golden Rule for family relationships:

One must die to self and live for the other

Genesis 2:24 Write it down:

How does this affect the closeness of the husband and wife? (Consider the closeness within the Trinity)

What does verse 24 say about this closeness?

An ideal family relationship:

1. Lets go of the past conditioning of our family
2. Maintains the goal of transparency

What is transparency and why is it important?

Write down Genesis 2:25

Refer to Genesis 2:25:

What does this say about transparency?

How does Genesis 2:25 figure in their relationship? (Consider how each felt about their roles and responsibilities)

The Attack on the Family

Anything God has established to reveal himself will come under the attack of the enemy. Satan's counter to God's revelation was to produce a distorted and dysfunctional revelation. The family system had to become dysfunctional. Satan's attack begins with deception.

This kind of *deception* <u>concerning what it takes to satisfy our needs</u> *is the central issue and root of all dysfunction* in our family systems.

What did Satan target with this deception of Adam and Eve?

What does Satan target with this deception of us? What is God's main provision for us?

Eve quickly focused her attention on the forbidden fruit as an answer to all that was missing in her life. To what did Adam focus his attention, when confronted with the deception? (Note that Adam was not deceived: 1 Timothy 2:14).

Read Genesis Chapter 3

Write down the last phrase of Genesis 3:1

Essentially, the same question arises in our own minds when we doubt what God has given us in Christ is really enough to satisfy us completely.

Genesis 3

The Attack Strategy:

1. Lead to negative thinking.
2. Focus upon what we cannot have.

Read Genesis 3:7-10

(Write down the verses)

What were the differences in the manner of deception? (Eve in verses 1-5; Adam in verse 6. What did Satan attack with Eve, and what did he attack with Adam?)

How does this relate to our dysfunctional behavior within the family today?

What emotions did Adam and Eve feel?
1.
2.
3.

Where do we see number one?

Where do we see number two?

Where do we see number three?

What did they do to try and make up for their situation? Why?

How was the revelation of God, through the family distorted?

What's going on in verses Genesis 3:8-13?

The Hope of the Gospel

Write down Genesis 3:15

The good news of what God does for us is that he sets us free from the bondage of personal and relational failure

What event does this forecast? Explain.

Write down Genesis 3:21

From the Christian point of view, what is symbolized by this text?

Look up Romans 5:12-21

Throughout the lessons that follow in this series, we shall emphasize this **one central theme** of the gospel of Jesus Christ, and how it sets us free.

Rebirth

Not in Adam

Now in Christ

Eternal Life:

A new identity; a new person created by God

The new identity: a child of God

Explain what the previous box means to you.

> **What God has done for us we couldn't do for ourselves!**
>
> God, himself, deals with their dysfunction, with all its shame, fear, and pride.
>
> God covers all our failures, with the righteousness of Christ.
>
> New creatures, in Christ, are free to love one another, with a divine love.

What is the difference between the inheritance we have in Adam and the gift we have in Christ?

> **In the joy and confidence of our hope, we can actually love one another!**

Foundation of Our Needs

Jesus Meets Our Personal Needs

Chapter 2
Lesson 1

Recognizing Our Needs

Needs must be met daily

If we are going to really understand who we are, we must learn to recognize our needs *on a daily basis*. Corresponding to the three basic components of man (body - soul - spirit) we have a set of needs to be met daily in order to live a healthy, functional life.

Our needs are defined on a physical, personal, and spiritual level.

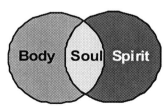

Everyone has needs that correspond to the three basic components of man.

Foundation of Our Needs - Jesus Meets Our Personal Needs

Below the three basic components of man are listed. Next to each, write in the need that corresponds to each basic component.

      Body _____

      Soul _____

      Spirit _____

Below, write each need (written on the previous page next to each basic componant) and then list examples of each need. One example shown.

Body air, water, food _____

_____

_____

> **More than physical needs**
>
> We are more than just a physical being, therefore, we have more than just physical needs.
>
> A common mistake, in trying to understand our needs, is to overlook the fact that we actually have personal needs.

> Everyday, we need to know that we are personally worthwhile in order to live and function on a personal level.

It is important to make **the distinction** between **our need to be loved** (a personal need) and **the need to love others** (a spiritual need).

Foundation of Our Needs - Jesus Meets Our Personal Needs

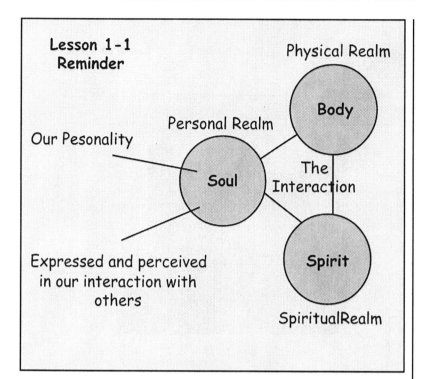

Study the chart to the right carefully

Incorrect assumptions about your needs

They are not being met
It is your responsibility to meet them
You are able to do so
It is someone else's responsibility
They are able to do so

In the follwoing chart, write in the basic needs of man. Rank the most important (for survival) at the bottom, up to the top, the least important (for survival).

To the left of the chart, write in each corresponding component.

To the right of the chart, write in each corresponding realm, or world.

Needs are Ranked

The ranking or importance of our needs is based upon survival, that is, what is necessary to keep the person alive and well.

This order is important. It cannot be reversed. Spiritual needs cannot be met until both physical and personal needs are met.

Foundation of Our Needs - Jesus Meets Our Personal Needs

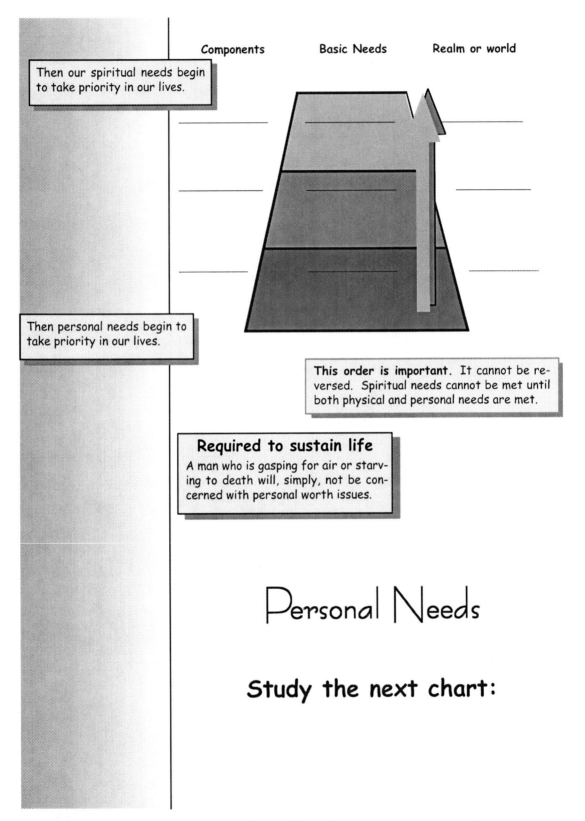

Then our spiritual needs begin to take priority in our lives.

Then personal needs begin to take priority in our lives.

This order is important. It cannot be reversed. Spiritual needs cannot be met until both physical and personal needs are met.

Required to sustain life
A man who is gasping for air or starving to death will, simply, not be concerned with personal worth issues.

Personal Needs

Study the next chart:

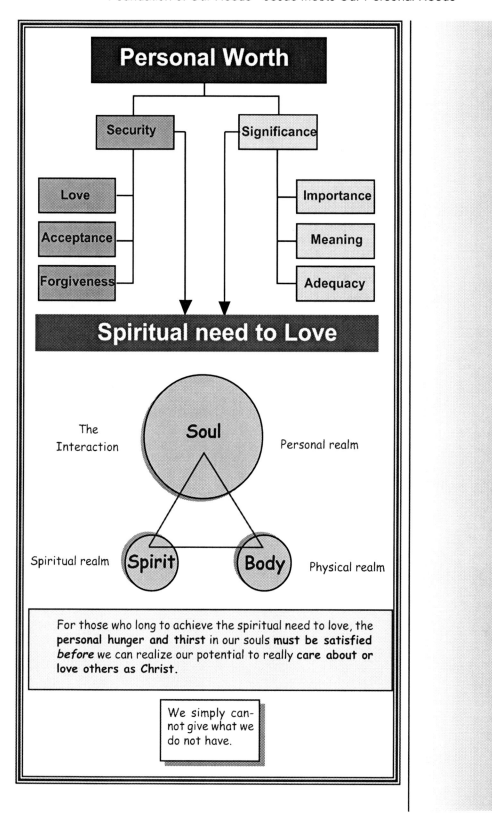

What are the two categories into which we can divide personal worth?

1. _____

2. _____

Why do we need to know we are secure and significant?

Explain why it is crucial to know we are loved **unconditionally**.

Explain why it is crucial to know we are accepted *just as we are.*

Explain why it is crucial to know we are *forgiven* for the past mistakes that continue to haunt our memories.

What does it take to experience personal significance?

Foundation of Our Needs - Jesus Meets Our Personal Needs

Importance

We are important, not because we do something, it is because we are loved unconditionally, accepted just as we are, and forgiven.

Adequate

God has made us adequate to cope with our circumstances.

Our **imortance** is derived from what is given to us, not from what we think we can earn.

The Bread of Life

Read John 6:49-54.

Jesus can satisfy our hunger and thirst for personal needs.

Insight

The sixth chapter of the Gospel of John reveals some astonishing insight into our own struggle to trust Jesus Christ as our personal savior.

Write down John 6:53

Explain how we get our **personal** needs, freely and constantly satisfied, by Jesus, on a daily basis?

_____

_____

How does Jesus satisfy our **eternal, spiritual** need?

_____

_____

How does Jesus satisfy our **physical** needs, with food, clothing and a home?

_____

_____

Foundation of Our Needs - Jesus Meets Our Personal Needs

How does feeding the 5,000 demonstrate, in the physical realm, what Jesus is able and willing to do in the personal realm?

How can we make Jesus into a "free lunch" and nothing more?

From the time we are born into this world we have been engaged in a daily struggle to meet these personal needs by our own means often regardless of what it takes.

Who do you trust for your security and significance?

Your self? Self change results in pride —becoming a pharisee

The world? The opinion of others

Trusting Jesus is crucial —despite worldly evidence to the contrary

God alone meets our needs —Adam's example

Complete and total identification

One with Jesus
Only, by becoming one with Jesus, would they experience the personal security and significance they needed, every day

Through such a vital union with Christ, *whatever is true of Jesus is true of them as well.*

Just as he is worthy
We are worthy
Just as he is secure
We are secure

FAITH

Believe we have become one with him

Believe we are secure in his love and significant in his plan

Trust that our union with Christ gives us a real sense of worth as persons

Trust our union with Christ liberates us to realize our true potential in Christ to love others.

Foundation of Our Needs

Our Union with Christ

**Chapter 2
Lesson 2**

In order to experience a true sense of personal worth, it is vital that we understand the very heart of the gospel message: *we have become one with Christ.* On the night before his crucifixion, Jesus sought to encourage his insecure and helpless disciples with a promise that reveals this gospel. Read John 14:20. In this lesson, we shall focus our attention on the biblical basis for personal worth, as revealed in the promise of Christ that we are in him, and he is in us. In short, we shall examine our union with Christ as it applies to our personal needs.

**PERSONAL WORTH:
The biblical basis**

Write down
John 14:20

Foundation of Our Needs - Our Union with Christ

The Promise

In what context did Jesus deliver the words of comfort expressed in John 14:20? Review John chapters 13-14.

What main motivation did the disciples share at this time?

What expectations did the diciples have of Jesus?

Who did they really think Jesus was?

What was Jesus telling them he was about to do?

In terms of worth?

In terms of prestige?

What was happening to their hopes and dreams?

Foundation of Our Needs - Our Union with Christ

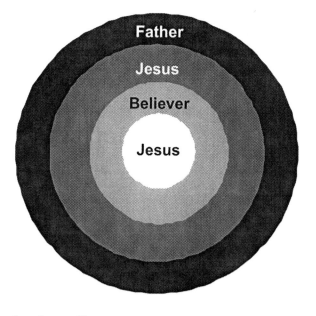

Describe the above diagram.

_____

_____

What is it about Jesus' words that gives us worth?

_____

The apostle Paul uses three different analogies in his letters to demonstrate the same promise. Believers are one with Christ as:

Ephesains 1:22-23

Ephesians 2:20-22

Ephesians 5:31-32

Write down Ephesians 1:22-23

Write down Ephesians 2:20-22

Write down Ephesians 5:31-32

Foundation of Our Needs - Our Union with Christ

The frequent use of the phrases, *"In Christ," "In him,"* or *"In whom"* in the New Testament, all reflect the basic promise that believers are in a vital union with Jesus Christ. It is from this union the believer draws incredible benefits of personal worth.

The Benefits

Was Jesus secure in God's love? _____
Are we? _____
Why? _____

Was Jesus significant in God's plan? _____
Are we? _____
Why? _____

Match the following statements with the appropriate verses. We are:

___ Loved unconditionally   **A** 2 Corinthians 5:17-21

___ Totally accepted   **B** John 14:12

___ Forever forgiven   **C** Colossians 2:9-15

___ Important as ambassadors   **D** Ephesians 1:3-6

___ Meaningful in ministry   **E** Philippians 4:13

___ Adequate in power   **F** Ephesians 2:1-10

What is the distinction between feeling worthy and being worthy?

Foundation of Our Needs - Our Union with Christ

Why is being aware of this distinction so important?

The Faith

In spite of the fact that Jesus has promised to identify himself with us, and us with him, in order to give us a true sense of worth, there are many other things we have learned to depend on for our personal security and significance. Before we are old enough to abstractly conceive that there is a God at all, let alone one who loves us, and gave his life for us, ***we have all been conditioned to trust in ourselves, others, and our circumstances to make us worthy***. As small children we learn to *trust in our own performance* to make us significant in this life. We also learn to *depend on the approval of significant others* to tell us we are loved, and, therefore, secure. These early learning experiences make it very difficult to later believe Jesus is the one who makes us secure and significant.

Read John Chapter 6.

What was the dissatisfaction that was in the hearts of the people to which John 6:66 alludes?

Write down John Chapter 6 verse 66

When we honestly ask ourselves what we depend on for our security and significance can we say we are any different?

Why not?

Foundation of Our Needs - Our Union with Christ

What factor allows us to develop and maintain a healthy sense of personal worth?

In Christ, we have all that is necessary to make us secure and significant. Apart from Christ we have nothing. The only thing left for us to do is to believe.

Why is this important for the Christian life style?

Understanding Our Emotions

Categories of Emotion

Chapter 3
Lesson 1

No attempt to examine ourselves is complete without understanding our emotions. Although difficult to objectively measure and define, emotions are obviously important to the quality of our personal and relational lives. In this lesson we shall describe the components and categories of emotions so that you may gain the necessary insight to effectively manage your feelings on a day-to-day basis.

Components of Emotions

The two main components of emotions are:

Define:

Define:

Defining Stress

```
                    ◄ ···· Prolonged stress ···· ►
  Stress
  Introduced
                         Resistance Stage
         Alarm
         Stage      Stress                          Exhaustion
                    Relieved                        Stage

Physiological Homeostasis | Normal body functions | Stress
                                                    Unrelieved
                                                    DEATH
```

Review the chart above:

Based upon your own experiences (consider both physical and mental aspects):

Describe how stress can be introduced.

Describe how the "Alarm Stage" comes into play.

Describe prolonged stress.

Understanding Our Emotions - Categories of Emotion

Describe how the "Resistance Stage" comes into play.

Describe the Exhaustion Stage

Describe how the "Exhaustion Stage" comes into play.

Read Matthew 4:1-11

How do Jesus' words, directed to Satan, reflect upon this understanding of stress?

The ABC theory of emotional cause and effect.
Review the chart below:

A Events Circumstances —Trigger→ **B** Beliefs —Trigger→ **C** Consequences Feelings

Understanding Our Emotions - Categories of Emotion

Considering A, B, and C; over which of these can we exercise the most control? ....

Why?

....
....
....

The real key to experiencing emotional freedom

> **Beliefs must be correct** so that feelings appropriately reflect the circumstances.

No one but you is responsible for your feelings.

Why or why not is this true?

....
....
....

BELIEVE "I AM WORTHY", IN CHRIST, DESPITE EVENTS AND CIRCUMSTANCES.

Categories of Emotion

To help clarify our thinking about our emotions we can categorize the various emotional states according to the following chart. Each term on the chart may be thought of as a category of emotional states.

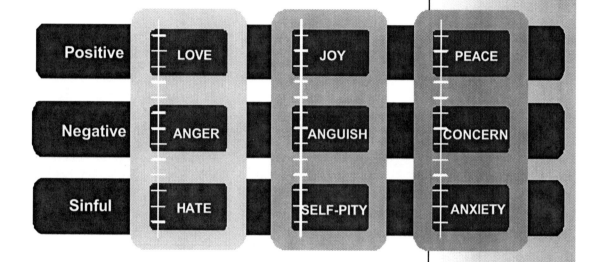

Sinful emotions:

Cause death

Limited death or poor health

Complete death of the person

Relational death

Understanding Our Emotions - Categories of Emotion

Describe the validity of each point listed.

Cause death

Limited death or poor health

Complete death of the person

Relational death

> **Negative emotions:**
>
> Are not sinful
>
> Negative emotions have an element of the positive
>
> Sin emotions have no element of the positive

Describe the validity of each point listed above.

Understanding Our Emotions - Categories of Emotion

Are not sinful

Negative emotions have an element of the positive

Sinful emotions have no element of the positive

SIN

Is an *emotional state which leads to death in some form.*

The Bible declares that anything leading you to death in any form is sin.

Romans 6:2

"For the wages of sin is death"

1

2

PHYSICAL
Psychosomatic disorders that bring on the death of a tissue, organ, or even the individual himself.

RELATIONAL
Relational death *destroys our relationships* to others.

The difference between negative and sinful emotions

Is God in it?

Have you lost control?

Understanding Our Emotions - Categories of Emotion

Write down the first phrase of Ephesians 4:26

Read Ephesians 4:26

What does it mean to be angry without sinning?

Write down Hebrews 4:15

Read Hebrews 4:14 - 16

What does it mean that Jesus can sympathize with our weakness?

> **The only way to stay away from death-producing sinful emotions is to exercise faith in the gospel that produces the fruit of the Spirit in our lives.**

Understanding Our Emotions

Emotional Healing

Chapter 3
Lesson 2

Sinful emotions such as hatred, self-pity, and anxiety can destroy us personally, and destroy our relationships with others. Although we naturally defend ourselves from such experiences through what psychologists call defense mechanisms (denial, projections, repression, etc.), these serve only to keep our rage, hurt, and worry out of our conscious awareness. The "bottled-up" emotions from past experiences will, sooner or later, find expression through psychosomatic disorders, personal dysfunction, and relational difficulties. In this lesson, we will begin to explore the ways we may cope with these sinful emotions.

From Hatred to Love

In Matthew 18 we find Jesus instructing his disciples about how to cope with the interpersonal strife brought on by jealousy and hatred. The occasion for this instruction was the question, "Who is the greatest in the Kingdom of Heaven?"

Read Matthew 18:1-14.

Write down Matthew 18:1-5

What would cause the disciples to ask, "Who is the greatest in the Kingdom of Heaven?" Think about the motivation involved.

Humility is needed to be the greatest

> Spiritual greatness comes when we, in childlike faith, trust Jesus to make us secure and significant.

Review verses 6-10 of Matthew 18.

Jesus uses some very strong language to teach us how we must handle the deception which keeps us from receiving our worth from him and loving others. He, first, gives a warning to those who offend others (verse 6). He knows that wounded people will wound others because of their own rage and bitterness.

What is the motivation, in the heart of the offender, that spurs the desire to offend others that is behind the warning Jesus issues in verse 6?

Why does this motivation exist?

What is the inward condition, Jesus refers to in verses 8-10, that produces outward acts of strife and bitterness?

What is the analogy Jesus uses to reveal the drastic measures needed to eliminate the hatred and bitterness that leads to offensive behavior?

This self-inflicted pain comes when we do what?

Why is doing this so important?

In verse 9, Jesus uses the term, "hell fire." What is the significance of this term (physically and figuratively)?

The actual process of eliminating the internal hatred that leads us to external strife is best described by the biblical concept of

Read Luke 23:34.

It is absolutely impossible for us to forgive others unless we experience

Why is this true?

Write down Luke 23:34

> To do anything less than forgive those who wound us is ultimately dysfunctional.

> It is absolutely impossible for us to forgive others unless we know we have received forgiveness ourselves.

> We need forgiveness for the hatred we have in our souls for others who offend us.

> When we realize we already have been forgiven in our unworthy condition, are we truly able to forgive others who trespass against us. Then, and only then, are we able to move from hatred to love for our enemies.

From Self-Pity to Joy

In the Garden of Gethsemane, Jesus, reveals the manner in which we may learn to cope with real pain, without becoming bitter and hateful.

Read Matthew 26:36-46.

In the following verses what is the overwhelming emotion Jesus must have felt? 36, 40, 43, and 45?

In revealing his anguish, what quality did Jesus reveal about himself compared to how we often tend to handle the pain in our lives?

Understanding Our Emotions - Emotional Healing

After revealing and sharing his pain with his disciples, what did Jesus do next?

In verses 39 and 42 what did Jesus reveal about his relationship to his father?

How is the account of Jesus' agony, more than a beautiful example of how we can face pain? Read Isaiah 53:3-6

From Anxiety to Peace

One of the most frequent phrases Jesus spoke to his disciples was, "Fear not."

FEAR NOT

✓ The disciples were constantly filled with anxiety, like the rest of humanity.

✓ He wanted to comfort them with his own presence and power.

Read Phillipians 4:6-9; Paul's prescription for worry.

How does Paul state we should handle worry?

What benefit will result?

What kind of frame of mind does Paul indicate we should maintain?

What should we be doing when worry, concerns, and anxiety come upon us?

Lord, grant me the patience to accept
the things I cannot change
The strength to change the things I can
And the wisdom to know the difference.

The Heart of the Problem

Traditions of Men

**Chapter 4
Lesson 1**

The Mind

The biblical proverb, "as he thinketh in his heart, so is he...," illustrates the importance of understanding the operation of the mind. If we are going to understand, much less change, our behavior or feelings, we must examine the underlying thought processes of the mind. Since our thoughts determine the quality of our emotions and our feelings determine our behavior, it is important to clarify and, ultimately, change our thinking, in order to affect any lasting changes in our behavior.

The Mind

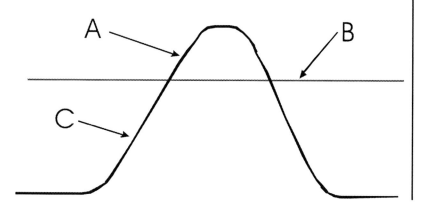

The Heart of the Problem - Traditions of Men

In the previous chart label the various parts.

        A. _____

        B. _____

        C. _____

What is self-talk?

Describe the subconcious mind.

Describe the conscious mind.

The Heart of the Problem - Traditions of Men

The Renewing of the Mind

The written word is a revelation of the grace and truth of the Living Word, Jesus. It is meant to lead us to true repentance and faith.

A revelation of the grace and truth of the Living Word, Jesus.

Read Ephesians 4:17-24

Verse 17:
The emptiness of dysfunctional thinking, of both the conscious mind and the subconscious mind.

Verse 18:
Dissatisfaction due to ignorance, and the inability to live in reality (hardness of heart).

Verse 19:
<u>Serious emotional and behavioral problems</u>: the overwhelming flood of sinful emotions which simply cast aside all good intentions in favor of doing anything to make one feel good.

Verse 22:
The biblical process of becoming healthy and functional.

Verse 23:
The critical step: this frees us to take on a brand new identity (clothe yourselves with the new self) in Christ

Define repentence.

Read Psalm 51:10

Write down ↑
Psalm 51:10

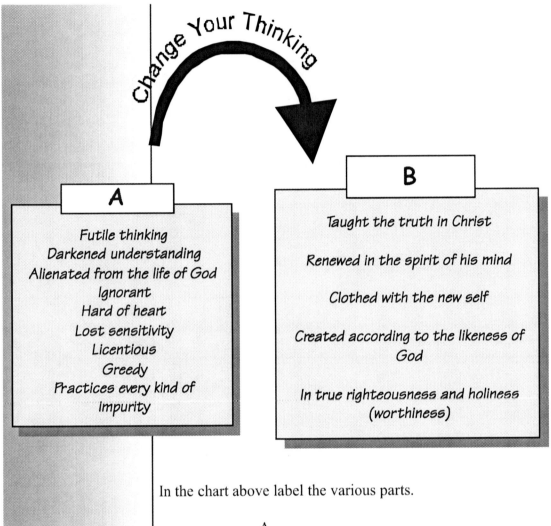

In the chart above label the various parts.

A. _____

B. _____

The Traditions of Men

The Traditions of Men

By "traditions of men" we mean the natural humanistic world view conditioned into each of us as we grow up. Later studies will fully demonstrate why these traditions are fundamentally wrong. For now, it is sufficient to note how Jesus exposes them as being the root cause of all our problems.

The Heart of the Problem - Traditions of Men

Read Matthew 15:1-20.
In verse 2, what kind of rule were the disciples disobeying?

In verse 7 Jesus calls the religious leaders hypocrites. Why?

Pay close attention to verses 8 and 9.
What is Jesus saying about the religious leaders of his day?

How does this apply to us?

Read verse 11. What is it about what comes out of the mouth that defiles a man?

What is the motivation behind the question in verse 12?

Write down the disicples question in verse 12

In verses 13-14, Jesus instructs his disciples to leave them alone, and then tells them they are the blind leading the blind. What is he talking about and how is this responsive to their question in verse 12?

What is the evil thought that is behind the desire not to offend and keep the traditions of men, even to the point of fear.

The Heart of the Problem - Traditions of Men

What is the true and good thought that opposes the evil thought and lifts us from being blind and being led by the blind.

The core issue of all our problems is this: we do not, by our very nature, believe we are worthy (i.e. secure and significant) because of Christ. *The evil thought, "I will be worthy if . . .," betrays our real motivation every time.* This evil thought, in all forms, must be recognized and challenged in our minds. Why?

The Heart of the Problem

How Problems Develop

**Chapter 4
Lesson 2**

In this lesson, we will combine all we have studied in previous lessons in a flowchart that describes how problems develop in our lives. In so doing, we hope to gain some practical insight into what is needed to be able to apply the gospel of Jesus Christ to our everyday lives. Living by faith in the gospel will not only improve the quality of our personal lives, but will also prepare us to relate to others in a functional, and more satisfying way.

Understanding our emotions is not enough. We must also understand the vicious cycle of trying to meet our own needs that lead to dysfunction and ultimately distruction. This vicious cycle is presented by the chart on page 61 (How Problems Develop).

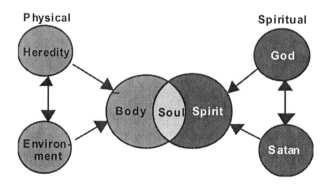

Refer to chapter 1, lesson 1 for the Structure of Man.

The Heart of the Problem - How Problems Develop

However, the effect of this vicious cycle begins by reviewing the Stucture of Man and the Hierarchy of Needs. At the bottom of the Hierarchy of Needs the need for worth and health, initiate the cycle.

Refer to chapter 2, lesson 1 for the Hierarchy of Needs.

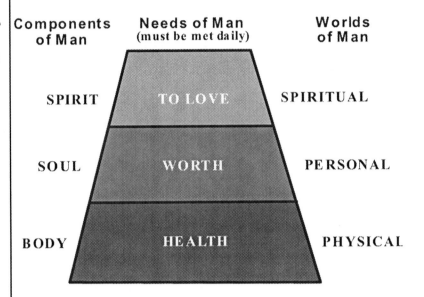

Why is the order of needs being met so important?

The Solmon Syndrome

At first glance the flowchart, on the next page, appears to be very complex, but it is really somewhat over-simplified. The proper use of this chart requires a willingness to look at ourselves, rather than to judge others, and to allow the Holy Spirit to gently, but firmly, teach us what he will. Please do not attempt to use this flowchart as a club to force others into changing; but rather, use it as a mirror to identify your own need to change. When sharing it with others, your personal experience, given in a spirit of true humility, will go far to encourage, rather than intimidate, the listener.

The Heart of the Problem - How Problems Develop

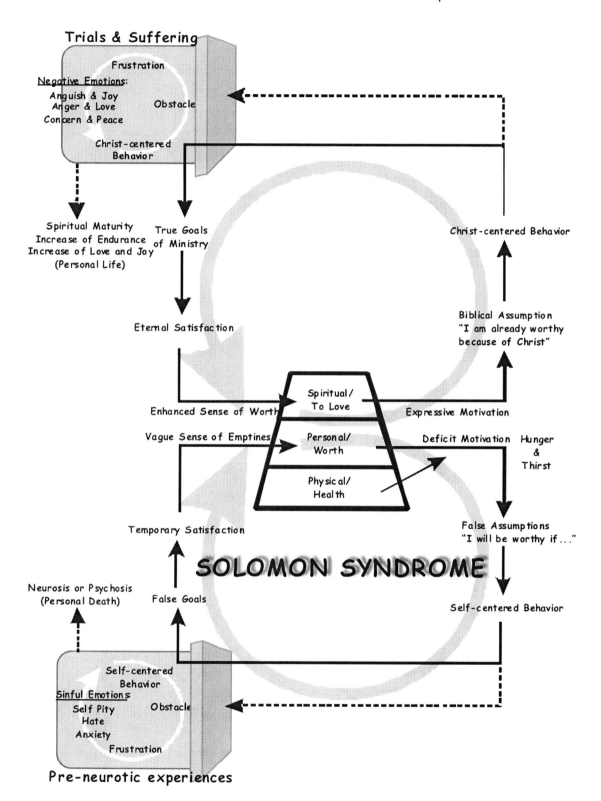

Deficit Motivation

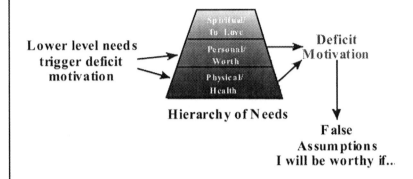

Define Deficit Motivation

What are some categories of needs that can develop into deficit motivations?

False Assumptions

Experiencing deficit motivation for worth as a person is common to all people. Every day we wake up with a hunger and thirst for worth because everyday we wake up as personal beings. Problems do not arise simply because we have deficit motivation.

The Heart of the Problem - How Problems Develop

How do problems develop?

What are the evil thoughts behind "I will be worthy based upon?" (See chapter 4 lesson 1.

What are some examples of false assumptions (based upon being worthy.)

What is the true assumption and why?

Deficit Motivation
↓
False Assumptions
I will be worthy if...
↓
Self Centered Behavior

Self-Centered Behavior

False Goals ← **Self Centered Behavior**

Self-centered behavior can often look quite altruistic, or religious, on the surface. We may do a variety of good works, and appear to be sacrificially giving of ourselves to others.

How do good works become self-centered behavior?

The Heart of the Problem - How Problems Develop

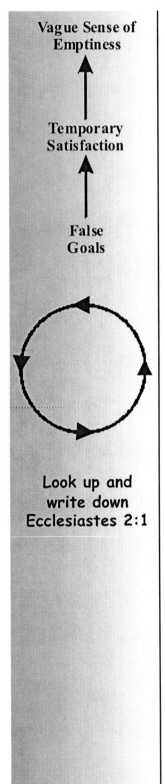

False Goals

A false goal may not be necessarily "bad" in itself. Why is a goal false?

_____
_____
_____

Temporary Satisfaction, And a Vague Sense of Emptiness

False goals, that cause us to seek the approval of others, always provide only a temporary sense of satisfaction. Why is this true?

Read Ecclesiastes chapters 1 and 2. Summarize what King Solomon did to achieve satisfaction.

What was his conclusion?

Hitting The Bottom

Anything that prevents us from reaching our false goals will also be the source of tremendous frustration. "Hitting the bottom" may be seen as the build up of intense frustration after repeatedly hitting an obstacle that keeps us from reaching our false goals.

False Goals ← | ← **Self Centered Behavior**
↑
Obstacles

The Heart of the Problem - How Problems Develop

Below are listed three means by which frustration is experienced. Next to each item write the accompanying emotion.

1. *Unreachable goals* _____

2. *External circumstances* _____

3. *Fear of failure* _____

After repeated attempts to overcome the obstacles, the frustration is so intense that our health needs become threatened, and we must begin to deny, distort, or even break with reality. What happens next?

_____
_____
_____

The help we usually want is whatever we think we need to get past our obstacles, and reach our false goals. What does this mean?

_____
_____
_____

What chief means do we often use to reach our false goals?

_____
_____

The Heart of the Problem - How Problems Develop

The Truth Shall Set You Free

The biblical approach to dealing with our obstacles is radically different from the secular. The Bible calls us to repentance; to change our thinking. In terms of the Solomon Syndrome chart, we are called to do what two things?

1

2

Every time we experience one of the emotions that leads to death (hatred, self-pity, anxiety) we come to what conclusion?

Define neurosis.

Define psychosis.

Read John 8:31-32.

What is the truth that sets us free?

Write down John 8:31-32.

67

Extra notes

Our True Identity

God's Regeneration Program

**Chapter 5
Lesson 1**

The core issue of our personal problems is traced back to the false assumptions we hold concerning what it takes to make us worthy. Since the false assumptions are so natural to us it is very difficult to even recognize, much less trust, the biblical assumptions concerning our worth.

The Need For The Gospel

In the first two and one half chapters of Romans the apostle Paul proves that all people are in need of the gospel of Jesus Christ.

Read Romans chapters 1-3.

List the charactetistics that Paul gives about human nature.

Beliefs	Behaviors

What are the dysfunctional uses of the organs of speech that Paul lists?

Summarize Paul's conclusion about the conditon and state of man.

Within this section Pauls tells us several purposes of the law. State them in your own words.

1.

2.

3.

What does Paul state about the adequacy of the law to make us right with God?

_____

_____

Read Galatians 2:16-21
What does Paul say here about the law?

_____

_____

Read Galaatians 3:10-13
What does Paul say here about the law?

_____

_____

Read Galatians 3:10-13, 24
What does Paul call the law (see verse 13 and 24)? Explain this.

_____

_____

Receiving God's Righteousness

Based upon the previous references what do we deserve?

_____

Read Romans 6:23?

Instead what do we get?

_____

Reread Romans 3:19-24 and Galatians 2:16.
How do we get it?

_____

Rightousness is a gift

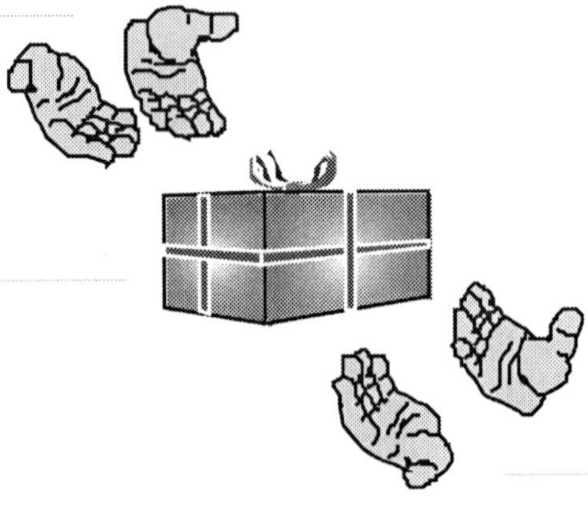

Enter labels is the blank spaces next to the illustration above

Describe the righteousness of God which becomes our righteousness.

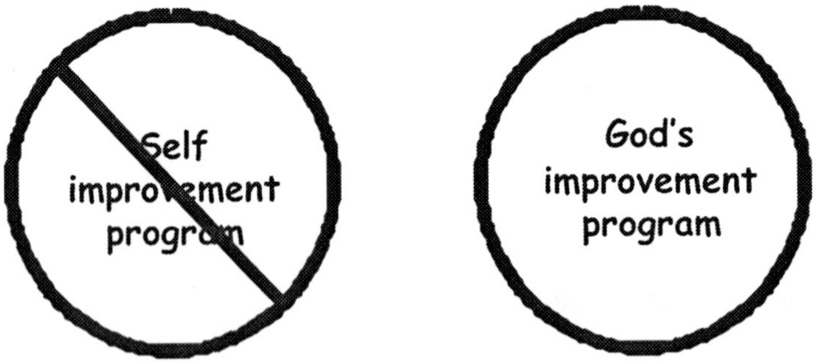

⊘ Self improvement program   God's improvement program

Our True Identity Identity - God's Regeneration Program

A _____

B _____

C _____

D _____

Based upon the text, label the above blanks.

Describe each.

A.

B.

C.

D. _____

God's Regeneration Program

The total gospel for believers is more than the fact that we have been saved from the guilt, and penalty of our sin. It also the fact that we are now being saved from the habit, dominion and power of sin in our lives.
Read Romans 6-8.

Since believers are really a brand new righteous person still living in a body that also houses a sinful nature, we are not surprised to find an intense inner conflict.

Describe this inner conflict.

_____
_____
_____

Read Romans 6:1-4, 6:11
What does this say about the biblical view of the inner conflict?

_____
_____
_____

Listed on the next page are some concepts along with biblical references in the sidebar. Match each concept with a biblical reference. There is more than one reference for each concept.

The life of Christ.

- Colossians 1:27
- Colossians 2:6
- Galatians 2:20
- 1 Corinthians 2:9-16

Lived by grace through faith.

- Ephesians 4:17-23
- Philippians 1:21
- Galatians 2:21
- Galatians 3:3
- Galatians 5:16
- Philippians 2:5-9
- Romans 12:2

Directed by the mind of Christ.

In Christ, We Are:

Loved	John 15:9; Rom. 5:5-8; 8:35-37; Eph. 2:4; 3:17-19
Accepted	Eph. 1:5-6; 2:13,19-22; Col. 1:22; Gal. 4:4-7; Rom. 8:14-17; 12:4,5; 1 Cor. 12:18-27
Forgiven	Rom. 8:1; Eph. 1:7; 2 Cor. 5:21; Col. 1:12-14; 2:13,14; 1 John 1:8-2:2
Important	John 15:5-8; 16; Eph. 2:10; 4:1-3, 11-16; Rom. 8:28,29; 1 Thes. 2:4; 5:14; Phil. 3:13,14
Adequate	1 Cor. 15:57,58; Eph. 3:20,21; 6:10; Phil. 1:6; 4:13
Needed	Rom. 15:1-7; John 13:34,35; 2 Cor. 1:3,4; Gal. 6:1,2; 1 Cor. 12:4-7

Our True Identity

The Promise of Victory

**Chapter 5
Lesson 2**

The Faith: Dead to Sin Alive to God

Based upon the fact that we are joined to Christ in his death, burial and resurrection, all believers are commanded to count on the fact that they are dead indeed to sin and alive to God. To use other terms, *we are urged to change the false assumptions about ourselves to biblical assumptions concerning who we really are in Christ.*

What is the central issue of faith?

In terms of our identity (who we are), what does God do to make us worthy?

Write down Romans 6:11

Our Identity - The Promise of Victory

Why does this make us worthy, consider the characteristics of our new identity?

In Romans 6:12-14 the apostle Paul outlines two distinct life-styles in which we may live. What are they?

1.

2.

What is the key factor that distinquishes one from the other?

When Paul discusses allowing sin to reign, it is neither a behavior nor a feeling. What is it?

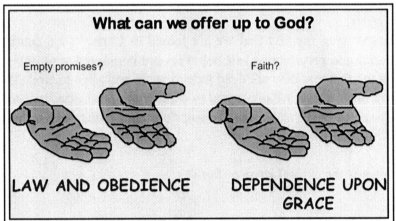

More Bible Study?
More Worship?
More Witnessing?
More Giving?

Are these characteristics of the Christian life-style?

Why or why not?

Often we believe the loss of our new found (or restored) joy and peace implies that it is somehow due to our conduct as a Christian. What is the danger in this kind of thinking?

The Lifestyle of grace

Faith → Hope → Love

The Lifestyle of grace

Fear → Guilt → Pride

Our Identity - The Promise of Victory

Read Ephesians 2:1-3. Contained here is a description of walking according to the world. List the characteristics mentioned.

Read Ephesians 2:4-13.
This is God's answer to this problem. Focus on verse 5. How does God save us from the habit and power of sin?

By what means do we actually put off the old-self and put on the new-self?

The Mirror

The Old and New Covenants

**Chapter 6
Lesson 1**

The promise that sin shall not have dominion over us is good news for all who are struggling with personal and relational problems.

The root of all our dysfunction and that which blocks our hope can be traced to what factors?

What is our only responsibility in the process of being saved?

In this study we will explore more fully how we are changed by the lifestyle of grace by contrasting it with the natural lifestyle of law. This contrast is not simply a matter of religious preference or a subject of theological debate. It is ultimately a contrast between freedom and bondage, and life and death.

What does it mean to be joined to Christ?

The Mirror - The Old and New Covenants

What does being "set free" mean and what is its purpose?

What does it mean that the old man was put to death, and the new man was raised to life?

The Old and New Covenants

Write down 2 Corinthians 3:5

Read 2 Corinthians chapter 3.
Describe the main theme of this chapter.

Define the biblical use of the term covenant.

The Old Covenant is a contract of _____
What does this mean?

The New Covenant is a contract of _____
What does this mean?

The Mirror - The Old and New Covenants

List several characteristics of the Old Covenant.

_____

_____

List several characteristics of the New Covenant.

_____

_____

What is the main Old Testament event associated with the Old Covenant?

_____

Read Jeremiah 31:31-34.

What does God promise he will do?

I will _____
I will _____
I will _____
I will _____
I will _____

How does God compare this new agreement to the former?

_____

_____

Review the "I will" list above. Describe your understanding, and your feelings.

Understanding: _____

_____

Feelings: _____

_____

The Letter Kills, The Spirit Gives Life

The life and death contrast between the lifestyles of law and grace is demonstrated by the effect each has on the believer. Paul uses the term "letter" to refer to the lifestyle under the Old Covenant of law.

Read Romans 2:29, Romans 7:6, and 2 Corinthians 3:6.
First read in the King James or New King James version and then in the NIV. Note the difference in words, but the same meaning.

What contrast is drawn between the lifestyle of law and the lifestyle of grace?

Besides causing us personal frustration or spiritual pride, *relying upon the letter of the law simply does not work to produce a righteous life.*

If we are not to be led by the law, by what are we led?

Read Galatians chapter 3.

What purpose does the law serve?

The Mirror - The Old and New Covenants

From Glory to Glory

Read 2 Corinthians chapter 3.

The remaining verses of 2 Corinthians chapter 3, complete the contrast between law and grace in terms of glory. The contrast between law and grace is viewed as the difference between glory and more glory, in its fullest meaning.

In what way is the law viewed as glorious?

_____
_____
_____

What does Paul describe as the ministry of death?
Why? _____
_____

What does Paul say about the glory of the law regarding its status?

_____
_____
_____

How does Paul contrast the glory of the ministry of the law (old covenant), with the glory of the ministry of the Spirit (new covenant)?

_____
_____
_____

What does Paul says about the minds of those who depend upon the law for righteousness and right living? _____
_____

The Mirror - The Old and New Covenants

The practical application of this contrast between law and grace is summarized in the last verse of the chapter. Explain.

What effect does the illumination of the Holy Spirit have on our minds?

What does the expression, "glory to glory" mean?

The Mirror

Slaves to Righteousness

Too Good To Be True

**Chapter 6
Lesson 2**

Jeremiah 31:33-34

> ³³ "This is the agreement I will make with the people of Israel at that time," says the LORD: "I will put my teachings in their minds and write them on their hearts. I will be their God, and they will be my people."
> ³⁴ "People will no longer have to teach their neighbors and relatives to know the LORD, because all people will know me, from the least to the most important," says the LORD. "I will forgive them for the wicked things they did, and I will not remember their sins anymore." (NCV)

The good news that sin shall not have dominion over us because we are not under law, but under grace. What does this mean?

Write down Romans 6:14

The Mirror - Slaves to Righteousness

This good news is almost too good to be true and difficult to accept. Why?

Look at the Jeremiah 31 verses on the preceding page. How does this describe God's responsibility toward our sin problem?

Write down Romans 6:15

Why is the gospel of grace *not* an open invitation to sin?

What is the difference of living in the dominion (reign) of sin verses living in the dominion (reign) of righteousness?

Servants of Righteousness or Sin?

Considering the previous question, what term does Paul use to desribe our relationship to each particular dominion?

What are the ramifications of this term in our lives?

The Mirror - Slaves to Righteousness

> *I say then: Walk in the Spirit, and you shall not fulfill the lust of the flesh.* - For the flesh lusts against the Spirit, and the Spirit against the flesh; and these are contrary to one another, so that you do not do the things that you wish. But if you are led by the Spirit, you are not under the law
>
> Galatians 5:16-18

Describe the struggle that Paul tells us about in Galatians 5:16-18.

What is going on between the flesh and the Spirit?

What is the result?

Read Ephesians 2:1-10.

We were once _____, but now we are _____.

In the former state how did we go about life?

What does Paul say in verses 3 about our *natural* way of life?

Who is responsible for our new condition?

What term does Paul use to define our new condition in relationship to God (verse 10)?

The Mirror - Slaves to Righteousness

What is the implication for us?

The keys to the lifestyle of grace

- Remember your true identity
- Count on the fact that we are dead to sin and alive unto God
- Count on the fact that we have been made slaves to righteousness

---

How does Paul call upon us to realize our new identity?

How do we offer or present ourselves to God as slaves or servants of righteousness?

Why is this a matter of faith and not of deeds?

Eternal Life Through Jesus

Read Romans 6:20-23.

In the closing verses of the chapter, Paul contrasts the result of being a slave to sin to the result of being a slave to righteousness. What does he mean by the fruit of each lifestyle?

What is the significance of the term "wages" in verse 23. (Also see Romans 4:4-5)?

Why do you think of God's word as a mirror of our real identity?

Read Romans 6:13-14

What drives us to live "as those that are alive from the dead"

Extra Notes

Who Shall Deliver Me?

Dead to the Law

Chapter 7
Lesson 1

The promise that sin (with all its dysfunction) shall not have dominion over us is based upon the fact that we are no longer under the law, but under grace. Having considered and dealt with the natural tendency to pervert this great promise into a license to sin, *Paul goes on to explain the basis of this promise as our death to the law.* By grace through our faith in the gospel message the old, sinful, dysfunctional person we were by nature was crucified, and buried with Christ, and a new person was raised up with Christ to be a servant of righteousness. To the extent that we accept this new identity by faith we are progressively changed into the image of Christ. To continue to live, and grow in the grace of God requires that we understand what it means to be *dead, not only to sin, but also to the law.*

Once we understand who we are in Christ, and what that identity includes often our tendency is to live for Christ, but under the law. As Christians we try hard to be obedient, trying to please God forever missing the full impact of grace.

What is the realtionship between the old dysfunctional person we were and the new person that was raised up with Christ?

Who Shall Deliver Me? - Dead to the Law

Read Romans chapter 7:1-3.
What does this analogy of Paul's illustrate?

What is the requirement that breaks the chains of the law?

See chapter six of Alpha textbook.

Name the six types of law that entangle our lives that can rob us of our freedom in Christ. Along with each give the demands and expectations that apply heavy burdens.

1. Parents

2. Social

3. Peer

4. Civil

5. God's

6.

Expectations
Law
In addition to the Old Testement laws
there are over 1000 New Testement laws.

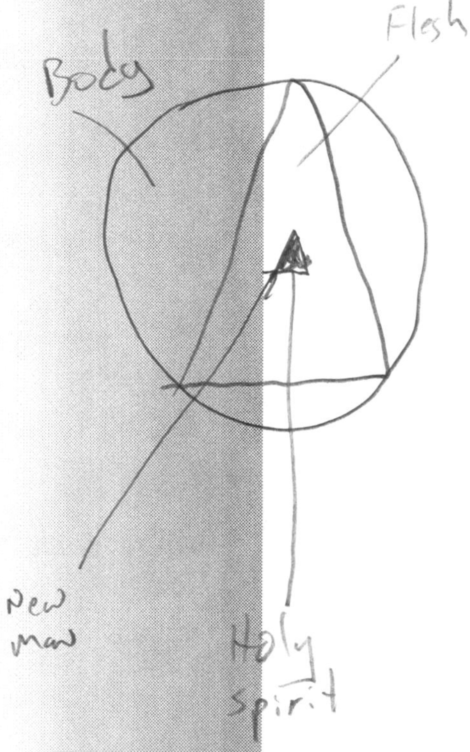
Flesh
Body
New man
Holy Spirit

Who Shall Deliver Me? - Dead to the Law

Write down Matthew 11:28

Look up Matthew 11:28

How do Jesus' words relate to this problem? What does he mean by "rest"?

The Believer's Death to the Law

Write down Romans 7:4

Read Romans 7:4-6

How does this shed light on the analogy of verses 1-3?

To "whom" or what were we "naturally" married?

What happened to the old person we were and what impact does that have on our former marriage and why?

Who Shall Deliver Me? - Dead to the Law

Our union with, or marriage to Christ means that we receive His "name," or identity which is, among others, the Righteous One. What impact or meaning does this imply?

Read Romans 6:6-10.
Explain how this relates to Romans 7:1-6

Our freedom from the "Old Man," and the law which dominated that "Old Man" is said to be accomplished in the death of Christ on the cross.

Read Colossians 2:10-14.
What does this say about our former lives and our new ones and about the means for transitioning between the two?

Write down Colossians 2:19-14

What is "the circumcision made without hands" (NKJV) or "not with a circumcision done by the hands of men" (NIV)?

Who Shall Deliver Me? - Dead to the Law

What is the "handwriting of requirements that was against us, which was contrary to us" (NKJV) or "the written code, with its regulations, that was against us and that stood opposed to us" (NIV)?

Read Galatians 3:22-23.
What is the relationship between law and faith?

How does this relate to Romans 7:1-5?

The Purpose of the Law

Read Romans 7:7-13.
What does Paul mean in verse 7 about knowing what sin is?

In verse 7:8-10 what does Paul mean by "For apart from the law sin *was* dead?" (NKJV).

What does Paul mean in verse 12, i.e. the two purposes of the Law?

Explain how each of the following is true?

When we turn to Christ in faith, the purpose of the law is fulfilled.

We live our lives by grace, not law, through faith in our union with Christ.

Once the purpose of the law is served in our lives, it has no more purpose; it has done it's job.

Extra Notes

Who Shall Deliver Me?

Conflict without Condemnation

Chapter 7
Lesson 2

It is indeed a struggle to live the Christian life. There are demands and expectations everywhere. As we struggle to live up to these demands and expectations we develop a poor (and unbiblical) self-image. Due to circumstances or relational problems, we begin to view ourselves as being less secure or significant as a person.

Read Romans 7:14-25. describe the nature of Paul's struggle.

_____
_____
_____

Mistaken Identity

How does Paul's confusion contribute to his poor image?

_____
_____
_____

We all struggle with our self-image. What are the factor's which can contribute to a poor self-image? Focus on performance.

Why is the attitude portrayed in the cartoon incorrect?

> I am worthless due to my sin exposed in by the law.

What conclusion is Paul drawing in verse 16?

What has Paul lost sight of at this point? (See Romans 6:11) In what kind of stinking thinking was Paul engaged?

Where does Paul think of himself as his flesh?

Where does Paul think of himself as the new man?

All Christians must grasp the same realization, it is our true identity that counts in spite of our poor performance.

The Distinction in Identity

Flesh

- Genetic Inheritance
- Positive & Negative Experiences
- Physical Body
- New Person (Inner Man)

Old   **New**

In verses Romans 7:17-20 Paul makes an important distinction between his true identity as a believer in Jesus Christ, and the nature of indwelling sin. In the figure above this distinction is illustrated by the difference between the inner and outer triangles within the same circle.

Explain the factors presented in the previous diagram that affect the struggle within each of us.

Write down Romans 6:6

Read Romans 6:6.
What does this say about the truth about us?

Write down Romans 6:17

Read Romans 6:17?
What does this say about the truth about us?

The Need For Deliverance

Read Romans 7:21-24.
What does this say about Paul's will power and its sufficiency to enable him to overcome the habit and power of sin?

What does Paul's anguish express in verse 24 tell us?

How does this summary of Paul's conflict apply to all believers?

Read Romans 8:1.

How does this bring light on the struggle Paul has just summarized in the latter verses of Romans 7?

What is the key word in Romans 8:1? Why?

How does this help you with your relationship with God?

How does this relate to your identity, i.e. the answer to the question, "Who am I?"

> **Write down Romans 8:1**

Extra Notes

Romans
6:11

Sin
Trust in God to love others

Salvation by Grace

The Freedom of the Spirit

**Chapter 8
Lesson 1**

AN OVERVIEW OF ROMANS 8

What a relief it is to know that we are under no condemnation as Christians; even in the middle of our struggle against our own sinful impulses of the flesh. *If there is any one message that is needed by the church today, it is the good news that Christians are not guilty, and should not fear the wrath and condemnation of God.*

No Condemnation

Read Romans 7:21-24

Describe how you relate to this frustration.

_____
_____
_____
_____

Read Romans 6:3-11.
How do these verses relate to these frustrations?

Read Romans 6:17-18
Explain verse 17 and the idea of "obeyed from the heart" (nkjv) or "wholeheartedly obeyed" (niv) in its relationship to verse 18.

Relate our union with Christ, crucified, and the concept of the "old man" in contrast to the "new man."

How does the indwelling principle of sin (i.e. the flesh) interplay with the "new man"?

Why is the degree of security we experience directly proportional to the extent we realize, and accept, in faith, the fact of our new position "in Christ"?

Salvation by Grace - The Freedom of the Spirit

Read Romans 8.
What is the transition Paul alludes to as he takes the reader from chapeter 7 to chapter 8?

Read Romans 5:12.
This describes the initiation of the principle (law) of sin. Read Romans 6:23. This describes the condemnation from which we must be rescued.

Read John 3:5-8; 1 Cor. 12:13; Eph. 1:13-14, 4:30, John 7:37-39; 14:17.

Believers are not under condemnation and set free from the principle (law) of sin and death by the principle (law) of the Spirit of life in Christ Jesus. Explain the role of the Spirit in setting us free.

What is it that the law can never provide that the Spirit provides abundantly?

Read 2 Cor. 5:21.
How does God maintain justice (condemnation for sin), and mercy (forgiving sin)?

Salvation by Grace - The Freedom of the Spirit

Read Romans 5:18-19.
As a substitute for man and in contrast to Adam, what did Jesus accomplish?

Does this apply to the entire human race?

Does it apply to you?

When we trust Christ, what actually happens?

Read Romans 8:3-4.
How is the righteous requirement of the law fulfilled in us?

The Mind of the Spirit

Read Romans 1:18-32; 3:10-18; Gal. 5:19-21; Eph. 2:1-3; 4:17-19.

What do these verses describe?

Read Romans 8:3-11.
How do these concepts compare or contrast to the previous verses above?

What characterizes the difference between life in the flesh and life in the Spirit? Be careful with your answer. Focus on Romans 8:5-7. Also see 1 Cor. 2:13-14.

What are the characteristics of "life in the flesh"? Think of the focus of dependence for this life-style.

What are the characteristics of "life in the Spirit"? Think of the focus of dependence for this life-style.

How does the "mind of the Spirit" fulfill the law of God and please Him in contrast to the "mind of the flesh"?

Salvation by Grace - The Freedom of the Spirit

The Mind of Christ

Of special significance when it comes to the mind of the Spirit is the realization *we have been given the mind of Christ*. As noted earlier, if we are going to live a healthy functional life, we must learn *to base our worth as persons on biblical assumptions of truth*. These are composed of perceptions, thoughts and beliefs that *coincide with the "mind of Christ."*

Philippians 2:5-8

Let this mind be in you which was also in Christ Jesus, who, being in the form of God, did not consider it robbery to be equal with God, but made Himself of no reputation, taking the form of a bondservant, and coming in the likeness of men. And being found in appearance as a man, He humbled Himself and became obedient to the point of death, even the death of the cross.

List the characteristics of the mind of Christ.

_____

_____

_____

_____

_____

We *walk by faith not by sight*. In order for our behavior to conform to our true identity, it is essential that the Spirit renew our minds from the inside out.

Do these characteristics apply to you?

Salvation by Grace

The Call to Faith

**Chapter 8
Lesson 2**

The apostle Paul directs our attention to the person and work of the Holy Spirit living within each believer by describing the miraculous way that God is delivering His people from the habit and dominion of sin, and all its dysfunction.

Each of us experiences an inner conflict with the sin of our flesh. This a sign of what? Why?

_____

_____

_____

_____

Read Romans 8:9-13. In verse 10 it says, "but the Spirit *is* life because of righteousness." (nkjv). To whose righteousness does this refer?

_____

What provision is given to us that we need to be delivered from the bondage of our own flesh, that is our captivity to sin?

_____

_____

Salvation by Grace - The Call to Faith

You Are Not Your Flesh But Born of the Spirit

In verse 9 Paul writes. "But you are not in the flesh but in the Spirit" (nkjv). How does this make us think of ourselves? How does this affect our identity?

Read John 3:3.

What does this tell us of our identity?

In living the new life are the following true or false?

Are you just a sinner saved by grace?
Are you required to turn a new leaf?
Are you to take an inventory of your sins and try harder?
God is pleased when you try hard?
Your behavior reflects your true identity?
You should always try to be a good Christian?

How does being born anew and actually becoming a new creation affect the way you answer the questions above?

Salvation by Grace - The Call to Faith

Resurrection Power

Paul reveals the source of the power we need to overcome the sin nature of the flesh that wars against us. Read Romans 8:11.

He says we are promised that the same Spirit, that raised up Christ Jesus from the dead, who will continually work in us making our mortal bodies come alive with resurrection power.

How can the resurrection power of the Spirit renew our minds, comfort us emotionally, and empower us?

Living In The Spirit

The resurrection power in the Spirit promised to us is the key to experiencing the abundant life Jesus came to give.

Read Romans 8:13-17.
Regarding identity, what is the contrast made between the life in the Spirit and life in the flesh?

Read Romans 8:13-17

Because it is impossible to "just say no to sin," and considering these words, how do we avoid the trap of Romans 7 where Paul says, "What a wretched man I am! Who will rescue me from this body of death?" (nkjv) What is the means we use to "put to death the misdeeds of the body?" (nkjv).

Salvation by Grace - The Call to Faith

What one word summarizes our responsibility to live by the Spirit?

Read Galatians 5:5-6.
What two means do we use to appropriate the "hope of righteousness?"

What counts and what doesn't count?
Counts:
Doesn't count:

What does circumcision and uncircumcision represent in these verses?

Galatians 5:16-18.

I say then: Walk in the Spirit, and you shall not fulfill the lust of the flesh. For the flesh lusts against the Spirit, and the Spirit against the flesh; and these are contrary to one another, so that you do not do the things that you wish. But if you are led by the Spirit, you are not under the law. (nkjv)

How is it that walking in the Spirit enables us to not fulfill the lusts of the flesh?

Salvation by Grace - The Call to Faith

When we walk "in the Spirit," what is our responsibility?

Considering the answer above, the exact opposite would reflect walking in the flesh. What would that be?

What is God's responsibility in all this?

Extra Notes

The Comfort of the Spirit

Personal Assurance of the Spirit

**Chapter 9
Lesson 1**

What made Jesus so healthy and able to function so well in this world?

Is it true that everything that is true of Jesus is true of you? Why or why not?

Since we are under no condemnation, free from guilt, free from feeling guilty, free from fear, able to face God with boldness and confidence, and fully equipped, how does that relate to our relationship with God?

The Comfort of the Spirit - Personal Assurance of the Spirit

Does this same Spirit that assured and led Jesus and Paul now live in you? How do you know?

Personal Leadership

What does Paul mean by, "For as many as are led by the Spirit of God, these are sons of God?" (Verse 14).

What is the significance of the fact that Paul uses the Greek term "huios" for the translated term "sons?"

How are the "sons of God" motivated?

How are they not motivated?

What governs our conduct?

How we can hear personally from God?

Romans

For as many as are led by the Spirit of God, these are sons of God. For you did not receive the spirit of bondage again to fear, but you received the Spirit of adoption by whom we cry out, "Abba, Father." The Spirit Himself bears witness with our spirit that we are children of God, ⁷and if children, then heirs—heirs of God and joint heirs with Christ, if indeed we suffer with Him, that we may also be glorified together. (NKJV)

Read John 10:27
Write it down

What are the three factors to consider when you think you are hearing from God?

1.

2.

3.

Beyond these three what is the most important factor, the bottom line when it comes to hearing from God?

The Spirit of Adoption

Beyond the failure to trust God what other obstacle prevents us from hearing from God?

See Romans 8:15

Why do we fall back into fear?

What is the Holy Spirit's first and greatest job as the Spirit of adoption, as he relates to us?

> **Galatians 4:6-7**
>
> *And because you are sons, God has sent forth the Spirit of His Son into your hearts, crying out, "Abba, Father!" Therefore you are no longer a slave but a son, and if a son, then an heir of God through Christ*

The Comfort of the Spirit - Personal Assurance of the Spirit

The Fullness of the Spirit

Ephesians 5:18

And do not be drunk with wine, in which is dissipation; but be filled with the Spirit

How does Ephesians 5:18 relate to the concept of being filled with the Spirit?

Ephesians 4:30

And do not grieve the Holy Spirit of God, by whom you were sealed for the day of redemption.

In Ephesians 4:30 we are told not to grieve the Spirit? What does this mean?

1 Thessalonians 5:19

Do not quench the Spirit.

In 1 Thessalonians 5:19 we are told not to quench the Spirit. What does this mean?

Galatians 5:16

I say then: Walk in the Spirit, and you shall not fulfill the lust of the flesh.

In Galatians 5:16 we are told how to overcome the flesh? How does this work?

The Comfort of the Spirit

Facing Trials in the Spirit

**Chapter 9
Lesson 2**

The real test of our faith in the gospel of Jesus Christ always involves personal suffering. Nothing causes us to doubt our worth as persons as much as the personal trials we are called upon to endure in this world.

What does Paul reveal to us in the first half of Romans 8 about God's provision in the Spirit?

What connection does Paul make in Romans 8:17 and the earlier text in Romans 8?

Romans 8:17
and if children, then heirs—heirs of God and joint heirs with Christ, if indeed we suffer with Him, that we may also be glorified together.

The Comfort of the Spirit - Facing Trials of the Spirit

Why Me Lord?

Read Romans 8:18-23

What is the truth about suffering revealed by Paul?

Romans 5:1-5
Therefore, having been justified by faith, we have peace with God through our Lord Jesus Christ, through whom also we have access by faith into this grace in which we stand, and rejoice in hope of the glory of God. And not only that, but we also glory in tribulations, knowing that tribulation produces perseverance; and perseverance, character; and character, hope. Now hope does not disappoint, because the love of God has been poured out in our hearts by the Holy Spirit who was given to us

This is called an eternal view. What is meant by that?

Read Romans 5:1-5.
How does this relate to our suffering?

How is it true that regardless of why we must suffer, *we cannot possibly lose*?

> **2 Corinthians 4:17-18**
> *For our light affliction, which is but for a moment, is working for us a far more exceeding and eternal weight of glory, while we do not look at the things which are seen, but at the things which are not seen. For the things which are seen are temporary, but the things which are not seen are eternal.*

How does 2 Corinthians 4:17-18 put our current suffering into perspective?

Review and discuss the following chart:

DO NOT BE SURPRISED	(1 Peter 4:12-14)
—Because of union with Christ	(John 15:18)
—For the sake of Christ	(Phil. 1:27)
—As a testimony to others	(1 Peter 3:13)
SEE THE END AT THE BEGINNING	(2 Cor. 4:17-18)
—God's love	(Romans 5:3-5)
—Joy unspeakable	(1 Peter 1:3-9)
—Peaceable fruit of righteousness	(Heb. 12:1-11)
—Spiritual maturity	(James 1:2-4)
KNOW YOU CANNOT LOSE	(1 John 5:4)
—With trial comes grace	(2 Cor. 10:13)
—God is in absolute control	(1 Cor. 10:13)
—All things work for good	(Romans 8:28)
—More than conquerors	(Romans 8:37)

The Deliverence in Hope

Our suffering, our "groaning within ourselves" is tied directly to the concept of deliverance-in-hope or the hope of delivery, the "waiting with excitement" that is occurring.

The Comfort of the Spirit - Facing Trials of the Spirit

Romans 8:19-21
The creation waits in eager expectation for the sons of God to be revealed. For the creation was subjected to frustration, not by its own choice, but by the will of the one who subjected it, in hope that the creation itself will be liberated from its bondage to decay and brought into the glorious freedom of the children of God.

Since we can't hope for something we already have and perceive, what does this say about avoiding suffering. Is suffering something we can avoid?

What is the definition of biblical hope?

How does hope enable us to endure the trials of this present world?

Romans 8:28-30
And we know that in all things God works for the good of those who love him, who have been called according to his purpose. For those God foreknew he also predestined to be conformed to the likeness of his Son, that he might be the firstborn among many brothers. And those he predestined, he also called; those he called, he also justified; those he justified, he also glorified.

List some of the attributes of hope as presented in Romans 8:

What is the personal significance of Romans 8:28-30?

What are the four specific actions of God regarding his overall plan listed in verse 30, that give us hope

The Comfort of the Spirit - Facing Trials of the Spirit

More than Conquerors

If God is for us who can be against us?

Who will bring a charge against us?

If God justifies, who can condemn?

Who can separate us from the love of Christ?

What does it mean that we face hardships for his sake?

How can we be more than conquerors in the face of the hardships of life?

Romans 8:31-39

What, then, shall we say in response to this? If God is for us, who can be against us? He who did not spare his own Son, but gave him up for us all—how will he not also, along with him, graciously give us all things? Who will bring any charge against those whom God has chosen? It is God who justifies. Who is he that condemns? Christ Jesus, who died—more than that, who was raised to life—is at the right hand of God and is also interceding for us. Who shall separate us from the love of Christ? Shall trouble or hardship or persecution or famine or nakedness or danger or sword? As it is written:

"For your sake we face death all day long; we are considered as sheep to be slaughtered."

No, in all these things we are more than conquerors through him who loved us. For I am convinced that neither death nor life, neither angels nor demons, neither the present nor the future, nor any powers, neither height nor depth, nor anything else in all creation, will be able to separate us from the love of God that is in Christ Jesus our Lord.

Extra Notes

Another Comforter

Relational Ministry

**Chapter 10
Lesson 1**

Christianity is Relationships

Christianity is not a religion; it is a relationship. There are two basic aspects involved in this relationship. Name and describe them.

Upon what is our relationship with God based?

As we begin to enjoy *personal* health (as expressed in the needs hierarchy explained in chapter two, lesson two "Jesus Meets Our Personal Needs"), we can now begin to express our love for others. Why now, and not before?

The Call to Divine Love

It is now time to apply the gospel, that God has met all of our needs, to our relational ministry with others by beginning to love others like Christ.

> **1 John 4:7-11**
> *Beloved, let us love one another, for love is of God; and everyone who loves is born of God and knows God. He who does not love does not know God, for God is love. In this the love of God was manifested toward us, that God has sent His only begotten Son into the world, that we might live through Him. In this is love, not that we loved God, but that He loved us and sent His Son to be the propitiation for our sins. Beloved, if God so loved us, we also ought to love one another.*

How do we know God loves us?

What is the significance of the command "to love one another" when it is connected to the statement that God is love?

How is the kind of love we receive from God radically different than our normal concept of love?

How does the absence of significance and security in our lives affect our ability to love as God loves?

Another Comforter - Relational Ministry

Upon what is typical human love dependent?

God's love can be described in five categories. What are they and describe each.

1.

2.

3.

4.

5.

Another Comforter - Relational Ministry

The Source of Love

Discuss the two prerequisites for being able to love like God.

1.

2.

Our Supreme Example

Read John 13:1-17

In John 13:1-17, we find a marvelous story of Jesus loving His disciples with a divine love to the very end. This example gives us insight into just what it means for us to love one another with the love of God.

When Jesus had finished washing their feet He asked them if they understood the meaning of this lesson.

Name four points that we learn from this account about our relationships.

1

2

3

4

Another Comforter

Comfort in Relational Ministry

**Chapter 10
Lesson 2**

Christian Maturity

Immediately following the startling announcement that he would be leaving his disciples, Jesus gave them the central command for all relational ministry.

What is especially noteworthy about this commandment that made it a "new" commandment.

_____
_____
_____

What does Peter's response to Jesus' statement about a new commandment indicate?

_____
_____
_____

John 13:34-35
A new commandment I give to you, that you love one another; as I have loved you, that you also love one another. By this all will know that you are My disciples, if you have love for one another."

Read the exchange between Peter and Jesus in the following verses 36-38

Although much of our study has been devoted to learning what God has done for us in Christ, it is now time to learn what God will do *through us* to love others like Christ.

The Call to Faith

Refer to John chapter 14

The comfort that Jesus shared with these men is recorded in the fourteenth chapter of John, and is centered around the call to relational ministry issued to all believers.

What does Jesus' statement in 14:1 indicate regarding the emotional state of his disciples?

What do the words of Thomas, Philip and Judas (not Iscariot) in the following verses indicate?

In verse nine Jesus speaks to Philip, but also to all of his disciples regarding their emotional state. What is the significance of his statement regarding their personal needs?

Reflecting upon this entire section, what is the meaning of Jesus' words in 14:6 (aside from the fact that salvation is through Jesus)?

Another Comforter - Comfort in Relational Ministry

The Promise of Victory

Describe the shift in thought that Jesus initiates in verse 12 and the following verses.

Which words of Jesus show how he sought to raise his disciples to this highest level of needs *by directing their attention away from what they might receive toward what they could give?*

What are the works Jesus talks about?

What is miraculous about the effect we have on others as we live the gospel on a daily basis?

How is the concept Jesus put forth about greater works to be understood?

In connection with this promise of doing his works, Jesus goes on to assure us that whatever we ask in His name He will do it to

John 14:12
Most assuredly, I say to you, he who believes in Me, the works that I do he will do also; and greater works than these he will do, because I go to My Father.

John 14:13-14
And whatever you ask in My name, that I will do, that the Father may be glorified in the Son. If you ask anything in My name, I will do it.

glorify the Father. What is the meaning behind this?

What does he not mean?

Abiding in Christ

The Vine and the Branches

Chapter 11, Lesson 1

The Key to Living As Christ

According to Jesus' own testimony, the key to His miraculous life and ministry as the Son of Man was His union with the Father.

Why?

Where did his personal security and significance come from to fulfill his mission and lay down his life?

Abiding in Christ - The Vine and the Branches

John

5:19 ...the Son can do nothing alone. The Son does only what he sees the Father doing, because the Son does whatever the Father does.

8:28-29 ...You will know that these things I do are not by my own authority but that I say only what the Father has taught me. ...The One who sent me is with me. I always do what is pleasing to him, so he has not left me alone."

10:30-38 The Father and I are one."
... I have done many good works from the Father...
... because I said, 'I am God's Son'? I am the one God chose and sent into the world.
... If I don't do what my Father does, then don't believe me.
... But if I do what my Father does, even though you don't believe in me, believe what I do. Then you will know and understand that the Father is in me and I am in the Father.
(ncv)

What was this relationship issue that moved Jesus to speak words of comfort to His worried disciples in the upper room?

What means of assurance did Jesus promise his disciples that would enable them to realize they would be one with him?

To help us understand the practical meaning of our union with Christ, Jesus gave His disciples an analogy of the grapevine and it's branches.

What is the significance of this analogy?

Why does it provide comfort?

Abiding in Christ - The Vine and the Branches

Practical Abiding

John 15:1-8

I am the true vine, and my Father is the vinegrower. He removes every branch in me that bears no fruit. Every branch that bears fruit he prunes to make it bear more fruit. You have already been cleansed by the word that I have spoken to you. Abide in me as I abide in you. Just as the branch cannot bear fruit by itself unless it abides in the vine, neither can you unless you abide in me. I am the vine, you are the branches. Those who abide in me and I in them bear much fruit, because apart from me you can do nothing. Whoever does not abide in me is thrown away like a branch and withers; such branches are gathered, thrown into the fire, and burned. If you abide in me, and my words abide in you, ask for whatever you wish, and it will be done for you. My Father is glorified by this, that you bear much fruit and become my disciples. (ncvRead 2 Peter 1:9

The analogy of the vine is a very beautiful picture of our union with Christ and it depicts four reasons for hope for Christians. What are they? Describe each.

1.

2.

3.

4.

To help us understand what it means to live out the gospel on a daily basis, we need to learn how to do "the trip in." In simple terms what is "the trip in?"

Describe what Jesus meant by walking in the light?

Abiding in Christ - The Vine and the Branches

Bearing Fruit

Taking "the trip in" helps us to bear fruit, a concept introduced by Jesus in John 15, that summarizes his promise to us. How does this work?

What characterization illustrates the concept of bearing fruit. In other words, where should your attention be focused?

Natural motives are replaced by corresponding spiritual motives. What are they?

_____ is replaced by _____
_____ is replaced by _____
_____ is replaced by _____

A failure to abide in Christ makes us susceptible to all the relational turmoil and dysfunction of the rest of the world. In contrast to this what does Jesus promise?

Read 2 Peter 1:9

What is the significance of 2 Peter 1:9?

Abiding in Christ

Living in Christ's Love

Chapter 11
Lesson 2

There can be NO greater sense of personal satisfaction than that which comes from continually living in the love of Jesus Christ. For that reason Jesus encouraged His worried disciples by calling them to live out their lives within the context of His divine love. We can experience personal satisfaction and relational health only when we learn to live daily in the love of Jesus.

The Father's Love

In exactly the same way that God the Father loved His only begotten Son, Jesus, all of Christ's disciples are loved by Jesus. What are the 5 attributes of God's love?

1.
2.
3.
4.
5.

John 15:9-10

As the Father loved Me, I also have loved you; abide in My love. If you keep My commandments, you will abide in My love, just as I have kept My Father's commandments and abide in His love. nkjv

Comment on each:

1.

2.

3.

4.

5.

Jesus tells us that obedience to His commands is the key to abiding in His love just as He was always abiding in God's love by obeying His Father's commands.

What does this NOT mean?

What does this mean?

The ultimate purpose for both the analogy of the vine and the call to abide in His love is explained by Jesus in John 15:11.

What are the "things" Jesus speaks of and what is their significance?

1.

2.

3.

Each of the items listed on the preceding page, corresponds to one of the following. Write in the number above for each.

        Faith _____
        Hope _____
        Love _____

Define the biblical term "joy."

Jesus wanted us to understand, from the analogy of the vine, and the call to abide in His love, that He has left us here to love one another in His absence. How does Jesus define *divine* love?

John 15:11

These things I have spoken to you, that My joy may remain in you, and that your joy may be full.

John 15:12-13

This is My commandment, that you love one another as I have loved you. Greater love has no one than this, than to lay down one's life for his friends. nkjv

Ministry or Manipulation?

Picking up on Jesus' attitude we can draw a contrast between ministry and manipulation. We have seen the real concept of ministry in the section that relates to John 15:11.

How is the basic difference between ministry and manipulation revealed?

What are the three characteristics of manipulation and what is their significance?

1.

2.

3.

The Overcomer

The Ministry of the Overcomer

**Chapter 12
Lesson 1**

The Bible has a very special term for those who are believers in Jesus Christ and are abiding in Him. They are referred to as "overcomers" to emphasize their victory over the spiritual enemies of the flesh, the world system, and Satan.

In this lesson we shall examine the specific ways we as overcomers, as victors, as conquerors, as winners are going to minister to others.

The instruction given by the apostle Paul in 1 Thessalonians 5:14 provides us with a working outline for the relational ministry of all overcomers.

> *Now we exhort you, brethren, warn those who are unruly, comfort the fainthearted, uphold the weak, be patient with all.* nkjv

In the early church, by what were the leaders known?

_____

_____

The Overcomer
1 John 5:4-5

For whatsoever is born of God overcometh the world, even our faith. Who is he that <u>overcometh</u> the world, but he that believeth that Jesus is the Son of God? (kjv)

The Conqueror

For whatever is born of God conquers the world. And this is the victory that conquers the world, our faith. Who is it that <u>conquers</u> the world but the one who believes that Jesus is the Son of God? (nrsv)

The Overcomer - The Ministry of the Overcomer

Similarly, they were to be loved and respected by what?

Before the third century, what distinquishing factor was missing that is present in the church of today?

Warn the Unruly

The first level of relational ministry overcomers are called to is confrontational in nature.

To what does the phrase "warn the unruly" refer?

Specifically, to whom is Paul speaking regarding warning the unruly?

In your own words explain the importance of Galatians 6:1 when warning the unruly?

Galatians 6:1

Brethren, if a man is overtaken in any trespass, you who are spiritual restore such a one in a spirit of gentleness, considering yourself lest you also be tempted.

Comfort the Feebleminded

The second level of our relational ministry as overcomers has to do with giving comfort to those who are "feebleminded" or emotionally distraught.

What comfort does the believer have to offer the feebleminded?

How are we enabled to offer comfort?

What is often more important than what we have to say and why?

> **2 Corinthians 1:3-4**
>
> *Blessed be the God and Father of our Lord Jesus Christ, the Father of mercies and God of all comfort, who comforts us in all our tribulation, that we may be able to comfort those who are in any trouble, with the comfort with which we ourselves are comforted by God.*

Support the Weak

The final level of our relational ministry involves the personal support of those who are weak in the faith.

What typifies the thinking of these folks?

What characteristics do they exhibit?

> **Romans 14:1**
>
> *Welcome those who are weak in faith, but not for the purpose of quarreling over opinions.* nrsv
>
> *Receive one who is weak in the faith, but not to disputes over doubtful things.* nkjv

The Overcomer - The Ministry of the Overcomer

Based upon Romans 14:1 how are we to support the weak?

To what do the terms "opinions" and "doubtful things" refer.

The weak brother or sister will not be as accomodating. Typically how will the weak brother respond?

How do we respond to the weak brother or sister?

What technique can we use in responding?

List some descriptions of the weak in faith.

The Overcomer

The Overcomer's Church

Chapter 12
Lesson 2

Matthew 16:13-19

When Jesus came to the area of Caesarea Philippi, he asked his followers, "Who do people say the Son of Man is?" They answered, "Some say you are John the Baptist. Others say you are Elijah, and still others say you are Jeremiah or one of the prophets." Then Jesus asked them, "And who do you say I am?" Simon Peter answered, "You are the Christ, the Son of the living God." Jesus answered, "You are blessed, Simon son of Jonah, because no person taught you that. My Father in heaven showed you who I am. So I tell you, you are Peter. On this rock I will build my church, and the power of death (gates of Hades-nrsv) will not be able to defeat it. I will give you the keys of the kingdom of heaven; the things you don't allow on earth will be the things that God does not allow, and the things you allow on earth will be the things that God allows." ncv

The concept of relational ministry can not be fully understood apart from the biblical idea of the church.

What is the very first example of the church?

The Overcomer - The Overcomer's Church

To this church what did Jesus promise?

The Revelation of the Church

The first mention of the church in the Bible is recorded in Matthew 16:13-19.

What prompted Jesus into this discussion?

When pressed by Jesus about his identity, how did Simon Peter respond?

How did Jesus clarify Peter's revelation of Jesus' true identity?

How does Peter's revelation relate to the revelation we receive about Jesus' identity?

What are the cardinal principles of revelation?

What are the two contrasting words that describe what the church is and what it is not?

What is the role of the true church?

The Foundation of the Church

The term "church" is derived from a compound Greek word, "ecclesia," which literally means a called out assembly or group.

In his statement to Peter in Matthew 16:18 what did Jesus reveal about the church?

How does 1 Peter 2:4-12 relate to the concept of the church and the authority of Jesus?

What does it say about the nature of the members of the church?

Matthew 16:18

So I tell you, you are Peter. On this rock I will build my church, and the power of death (gates of Hades-nrsv) will not be able to defeat it. ncv

Come to the Living Stone!

Read 1 Peter 2:4-12

The Mission and Purpose of the Church

Based upon Matthew 16:18, what is the understanding of the power of the church over Satan and his fortress of Hell?

What is the purpose Jesus has for the ecclesia?

The Authority of the Church

Matthew 16:19

I will give you the keys of the kingdom of heaven; the things you don't allow on earth will be the things that God does not allow, and the things you allow on earth will be the things that God allows. ncv

How does the text of Matthew 16:19 actually illustrate the relationship of the church and Jesus.

Why is the real and true church referred to as "the Body of Christ?"

2 Cor 5:17-6:2
The Ministry of Reconciliation

So if anyone is in Christ, there is a new creation: everything old has passed away; see, everything has become new! All this is from God, who reconciled us to himself through Christ, and has given us the ministry of reconciliation; that is, in Christ God was reconciling the world to himself, not counting their trespasses against them, and entrusting the message of reconciliation to us. So we are ambassadors for Christ, since God is making his appeal through us; we entreat you on behalf of Christ, be reconciled to God. For our sake he made him to be sin who knew no sin, so that in him we might become the righteousness of God. As we work together with him, we urge you also not to accept the grace of God in vain. For he says, "At an acceptable time I have listened to you, and on a day of salvation I have helped you." See, now is the acceptable time; see, now is the day of salvation! nrsv

Extra Notes

CPSIA information can be obtained at www.ICGtesting.com
Printed in the USA
LVOW091958070213

319166LV00002B/12/A

9 781425 969790